Front cover design by kind permission of
www.Brightonwiccansupplies.co.uk

Other Books by Alan Faraway

Pictures in my Head
Natures Child

A note from the author:

I was asked by Brighton Wiccan Supplies to write some Pagan poems for inclusion on their website. A few months later I received a message from them asking if I was, (or had), written a book of Pagan poems as many of their clients have asked the question and they would like to give them an answer. This is what prompted me to write this book. I hope you enjoy reading it. I have tried to give some information in the form of verse, mainly for the benefit of those of you who are either unaware of certain elements or are relatively new to paganism. There is also a quiz in the form of a poem which I couldn't help myself from writing. I would love to hear feedback and am willing to attempt to answer any questions this book may prompt. Follow me on twitter @AlanFaraway. If you enjoy this, perhaps you might like to look at my other books, let me know what you think.

Thank you.

Alan Faraway

Table of Contents

Winter's Hand
Mother Nature (Turns the wheel)
Forest Walk
Green Man
Mist Morning
Spring
Autumn
Spirit of Night
The Wiccan Witch
Glorious Autumn Day
Children of Earth
Arianhrod
Sad Farewell
Spirits
Silver Moon
Nature's Sound
Silver Goddess
Halloween
The Owl
Young Sun God
My Pagan Wish
An It Harm None
Wicca Man
Aeolus
Artemis
The Gods of Olympus (quiz)
Athena

Pagan Ways

Upon my altar a crystal ball,
An athame, candles and chalice tall,
A pagan goddess, a pagan god,
All laid upon my altar cloth,
A bell to help me celebrate,
Offerings placed upon a plate,
My pagan tools I now display,
How I love my pagan ways.

I'll cast my circle upon the floor,
Then call upon the quarters four,
Earth, Fire, Water, Air,
The God and Goddess may join me there,
I may sing, or I may dance,
I may even dare to chant,
As pagan music softly plays,
How I love my pagan ways.

My ritual over, now time to seek,
I'm feeling light upon my feet,
I'll walk among the trees and plants,
And search for berries upon the branch,
I'll feel the breath of natures kiss,
At one with all is total bliss,
I wish I lived in bygone days,
To learn first hand these pagan ways.

Wheel of the Year

Imbolc marks the start of the year,
A time for all things new,
Winters hand now has passed,
And the skies are turning blue.

Ostara sees that daylight,
Triumphs over night,
A fertile time for all that live,
Reborn to the light.

Then we herald Beltane,
With promises of fun,
All upon the Earth rejoice,
At the flowers in the sun.

Litha is the Midsummer,
When a mighty battle starts,
The Holly King will take the crown,
And the Oak King will depart.

Lammas now or Lughnasadh,
For the harvest we give thanks,
Irish pagans, a holiday,
Now the corn is safely banked.

Mabon, the autumn equinox,
We give our thanks and praise,
For all the fruits and food we have,
To last through the winter phase.

Samhain, when the souls pass through,
On their way to the Summerland,
Remember well the departed ones,
And wave with upturned hand.

Finally we come to Yule,
Deep in winters grasp,
The snow may lay upon the ground,
But the icy hand will pass.

That's the pagan wheel my friends,
I believe this to be true,
May your year be all you wish,
And the spirits watch over you.

Imbolc

To the Dagda, she was born,
And wife to Bres, a Fomorian,
Her son Ruidan, in battle slain,
Brighid the goddess of eternal flame.

A patron is she to the blacksmiths craft,
Of wisdom, perfection and the healing art,
Brighid the goddess from a place called Kildare,
The triple goddess who's everywhere.

In days gone by, all through the night,
Nineteen nuns kept the flame alight,
The perpetual flame surrounded by hedge,
That no man may enter, lest he be dead.

Fiery arrow, her name it does mean,
This triple goddess, this mighty queen,
Her festival we know as Imbolc day,
When flames to her honour Pagans lay.

Foretelling the weather tradition demands,
On Imbolc day light fiery charms,
At sunset light lamps in the home,
In honour of Brighid, to maiden from crone.

Walk in the snow, if that's on the ground,
With your hand trace the sun, as you walk around,
For the seasons are changing, winter to spring,
And Brighid is with you, let Imbolc begin!

Ostara

God and Goddess unite as one,
Sow your seeds in Springtime sun,
As you grow through Warmer days,
Your beauty shows in many ways.

Youth, vitality, young to old,
Your journey is forever told,
The earth will sleep when Winter comes,
But awake with you in the warm March sun.

So banish darkness with your light,
Let all things grow as well they might,
And we shall look in adoration,
At the God and Goddesses creations.

Beltane

Sow your seed in daylights glow,
Sit in wonder, watch it grow,
Now that winters hand has passed,
And the summer sun has come at last.

For plants and animals, humans too,
Fertility brings us all things new,
So lift your eyes to celestial lights,
And celebrate on this Beltane night.

Leave what was in days gone by,
For love this day is riding high,
So view the world with eyes anew,
Beltane has come for me and you.

Litha

Litha heralds the longest day,
The Sun Gods' power soon will fade,
The Oak king soon will bear the crown,
And long summer days will soon draw down.

Rejoice all witches young or old,
Let love for all things now unfold,
For when the summer days have passed,
We'll feel the chill of winters blast.

Lammas Day

Rejoice with me on Lammas Day,
Reap the first fruits, bale the hay,
Give our thanks for harvest good,
Give our thanks to the great god Lugh.

Rejoice with me on Lammas Day,
Bake the bread and let it lay,
Upon the table, on the plate,
Let's give thanks and celebrate.

Rejoice with me on Lammas Day,
With hand fasting and joyous games,
And may Lugh's blessing always see,
You happy and loving, peaceful and free.

Mabon

And so it's Mabon time once more,
Nature in balance as was before,
Equal night and equal day,
The Sun God and Goddess soon will lay.

We give thanks for the harvest reaped,
As the Sun God travels to winter sleep,
And we look back on things we've done,
And make new plans for the year to come.

Rejoice, be happy for all things must die,
No need to weep, no need to cry,
For all things return to earth some way,
So let's give thanks on Mabon Day.

Samhain

Spirits rise this Samhain night,
And if by chance you see their light,
Bid them farewell with upheld hand,
As they travel to the Summerland.

Between our worlds the veil is thin,
The spirits may enter to speak again,
But fear ye not no harm they'll do,
They've merely come to visit you.

Leave some food upon the step,
So souls may eat or even rest,
For Summerland is far from here,
And you will send them in good cheer.

Samhain's a time for jokes and pranks,
And also a time to give our thanks,
For Samhain is our New Year's Eve,
And we'll celebrate for we believe.

Yule

Yule time is now upon us,
The longest night draws near,
Pagans will light the fires,
And a new king will soon appear.

The Goddess will be the great mother,
The Sun King will be reborn,
She will give birth to a lover,
The wheel once more will turn.

Rejoice at the mid-winter solstice,
Ye pagans throughout the land,
Light fires and honour the Goddess,
Be ye woman, child or man.

A Woodland Walk

If you've ever walked through a copse or wood,
How many times have you just stood,
And looked more closely at the trees,
At the berries or their different leaves.

The natural world has a lot to see,
Not just animals, birds or bees,
Or fish that swim in the oceans deep,
Or insects scurrying on tiny feet.

The different trees that you can see,
When you wander through a wood that's free,
The leaves and fruits, a vast array,
Will fall to ground and rot away.

But leaves return year on year,
And produce their fruit for creatures near,
Humans and animals on these will dine,
Given by trees in the woods you'll find.

So when you wander among the trees,
Take some time and you will see,
What mother nature's showing you,
Perhaps you'll see with eyes anew.

Deep in The Woodland

Deep in the woodland hear my call,
We'll meet by the loving tree.
Deep in the woodland we'll be free,
When you tie your hand to me.

Deep in the woodland they will come,
The friends both old and new,
Deep in the woodland you'll find love true,
When I tie my hand to you.

Deep in the woodland we'll be blessed,
When the Goddess shines on us,
Deep in the woodland and without fuss,
In the Goddess we will trust.

Deep in the woodland they will say,
We were bound in the ancient way,
Deep in the woodland in love we'll stay,
For a year and just one day.

Mabon Moon

Can you feel the magic,
That's in the air tonight,
Will you feel the magic,
When you perform your rite,
I hope the Silver Goddess brings,
The magic home to you,
As you chant and dance and sing,
Beneath the Mabon moon.

Can you see the magic,
The earth has given you,
Can you see the magic,
In the fruit within the hall,
I hope the second harvest brought,
The magic home to you,
As you chant and sing and dance,
Beneath the Mabon moon.

Mother Nature

When Mother Nature's happy,
The Green Man wears his gown,
And you can see the beauty,
From the flowers all around.

When Mother Nature's saddened,
The rain god she will call,
The sky becomes more darkened,
Then you'll see her tear drops fall.

When Mother Nature's angry,
Her wrath is plain to see,
Her hurricanes and tidal waves,
Will bring us to our knees.

So man thinks he's the master,
But that is not the case,
Cos Mother Nature will show herself,
To put him in his place.

And if man tries to take her heart,
He'd better think again,
'Because she'll rip his world apart,
And he will know true pain.

Trees

Trees are not just pretty things,
Dancing in the wind,
Or a place for birds to roost or nest,
And raise their young offspring,
Trees are so important,
It's time to realise,
Without these woody guardians,
We will not survive.

They give to us the oxygen,
We all need to breath,
They hold the earth together,
Their roots go deep and weave,
They clean the air around us,
Just as well they can,
'Cos spilling into the atmosphere,
The poisoned air of man.

If we destroy the forests,
Take away the trees,
I doubt that we will live too long,
Brought down to our knees,
We must stop destroying,
The beauty of these lands,
'Cos the biggest threat to us is plain,
The stupidity of man!

Rejoice at Litha

Gather Pagans cast thy spell
Harm thee none and all is well
Draw thy circle, couldron light
Praise the spirits of day and night

Offerings on thy altar place
Welcome love into thy space
Dance and sing let joy abound
For thou art standing on hallowed ground

Rejoice ye all the Pagan way
For Litha hails the longest day
So gather Pagans young and old
Remember ancient stories told

So gather Pagans cast thy spell
Harm thee none and all is well
The gods on high will come to thee
To all ye Pagans, blessed be

Shadows in the Night

Flickering fires casting,
Darkened shapes among the trees,
And somewhere in the evening sky,
A night owl calls to me,
And there among the heavens,
The moon is shining bright,
Bringing all her beauty,
Casting shadows in the night.

Silhouetted against the sky,
The treetops take on shapes,
Like Broccoli spears or cauliflower heads,
And some just tall thin stakes,
I look toward the sea of stars,
And the moon that sends her light,
To shine upon this tranquil place,
Bringing shadows in the night.

The shadows soon will fade away,
As daylight begins to creep,
And as the sun climbs higher,
The shadows begin to sleep,
But they'll return to comfort me,
When the silver moon shines bright,
And the sun departs the heavens,
To leave shadows in the night.

Ode to the Goddess

Stars shine bright in the blackened sky,
And cold winds blow and sting my eyes,
But the moon is bright and beckons me,
To praise the Goddess that I see,
And as I do so a warming comes,
To block the cold that chills my bones,
So I give thanks to this heavenly soul,
And my world is touched by her tender glow.

Silver Lady

Silver lady of the night
Bathe us in your beams so bright
Spread your wings and fly unseen
Give hope to others, let them dream

Silver lady high above
Goddess of our Earthly love
Blessed are we to have you near
Your light of love we hold so dear

With loving hands you guide us home
On this earth we're not alone
You'll be with us for all of time
Silver lady, mother divine

Summerland

When my life is done, do not grieve
For I'll return if you believe
And in my time among you here
I've learned of love and hope and fear

My soul will rest in another place
Far beyond the void of space
There I'll rest on warm soft sand
Till again I leave the Summerland

Three Moons

Three moons rising in my home
The maiden, mother and wise old crone
Gently guiding me each day
Teaching me the Pagan way

Three moons rising in my heart
Will never leave me, never part
But stay with me my whole life through
Spreading love from me to you

Three moons rising ever more
Keeping harm outside the door
Three moons deep within my bones
The maiden, mother and wise old crone

The Natural World

Let the sun beat down its blistering heat,
That warms the earth beneath my feet,
The waves break gently upon the shore,
The tide ebbs and flows for evermore.

Let the moon above with gentle hands,
Bathe the earth in silvery strands,
As a trillion stars in the heavens deep,
Twinkle and sparkle in gentle sleep.

Let the flowers turn their pretty heads,
Their yellows and blues and pinks and reds,
Dance and sway in the summer breeze,
That gently touches the tallest trees.

The goddess works in harmony,
With her lover to bring to you and me,
The wonders of the natural world,
With love eternal, arms unfurled.

I Married A Witch

When first I saw you, I knew not why,
You were so appealing to my eye,
You cast your spell which did not miss,
I fell in love from the very first kiss.

No matter what I tried to do,
My thoughts would always return to you,
A feeling I couldn't quite understand,
Whenever I felt the touch of your hand.

Now I realise what you have done,
You've cast a spell, I cannot run,
Our love will flourish without a hitch,
Because now I know, I've married a witch!

White Witch of the Woods

Walking through the woods one day,
A few years ago, in early May,
The morning sun was shining down,
Forming dappled shadows upon the ground.

I wasn't really thinking much,
Idly reaching out to touch,
A leaf perhaps upon a branch,
Or watch two squirrels playfully dance.

No one else was walking there,
I was all alone without much care,
Just taking in the scenery,
And the beauty that surrounded me.

The woods were silent, and a gentle breeze,
Not strong enough to stir the leaves,
Oh so softly kissed my cheek,
As the squirrels carried on playing hide and seek.

I turned around and suddenly,
A lady was in front of me,
Dressed in white from head to toe,
On her shoulders, a raven and a crow.

How old she was I couldn't tell,
I seemed to be held in a kind of spell,
I couldn't move, I couldn't speak,
The earth itself seemed to grip my feet.

The raven and the crow took flight,
I stood transfixed at this awesome sight,
They began to circle above my head,
And I didn't hear what the lady had said.

Then unseen hands were holding me,
And everything was spinning furiously,
Yet not one single leaf was stirred,
I must be mad, my brain inferred.

Then she spoke in a gentle voice,
I listened intently, I had no choice,
Her words were soft and very kind,
They put to rest my frightened mind:

She told the story of this wood,
Her name was Adaryn I understood,
I thought that's Welsh and meaning bird,
I remember thinking that's so absurd!

Why that thought came to my head,
When I should've been really scared instead!
But something told me I was safe,
No danger lurked within this place.

As she spoke I could plainly see,
Tiny insects within the trees,
Hidden beneath the woody bark,
Living quite happily in the dark.

I saw the liquid pumping through,
The veins of leaves and plant life too,
Pushed from the heart of underground bulbs,
And watched their respective leaves unfold.

She said we look but never see,
The magic and the real beauty,
Although we listen we never hear,
The sounds of nature so very near.

Through various visions I was led,
And all the while above my head,
The raven and crow circled endlessly,
Their beating hearts became clear to me.

At last they returned to the lady in white,
And I saw the woods in a different light,
The lady stood with her raven and crow,
Perched on her shoulders, eyes aglow.

Then they were gone in the blink of an eye,
I looked all around and noticed up high,
A raven and crow flying East to the sun,
I looked for Adaryn, but she too had gone.

Now when I walk on this magical path,
I hear Adaryn's voice saying "look with your
heart",
I've not seen her since, but wish that I could,
See once more the White Witch of the Woods.

Spirits That Rise

Spirits that rise in ageless flight,
Take my dreams into the night,
Take them high and far and wide,
And lay them at my lovers side.

Spirits that rise on unseen wings,
Ageless spirits of hopes and dreams,
Spirits that dwell on the plains above,
Take my heart to my true love.

Though darkened skies my come our way,
My love I know will never stray,
Let my lover know that I am true,
Spirits that rise I ask of you.

Natures cloak

Natures beauty is all around,
The gentle breeze makes rustling sounds,
As it wafts between the reeds and plants,
And their little heads do natures dance.

The sun beats down on grasses green,
And tiny insects can be seen,
Scurrying across the open ground,
Yes Natures cloak is all around.

Birds soar high in arial flight,
We watch them all in sheer delight,
As they swoop and turn, majestic things,
And in the dawn their voices sing.

In the fields between the cows and sheep,
The fox cubs run and dodge and leap,
All the while the sun shines down,
Yes Natures cloak is all around.

Mighty oaks and Ash grow tall,
And in their branches a Rook may call,
And squirrels climb their branches wide,
Within the treetops they will hide.

From caterpillars they have come,
To fly and rejoice in the warming sun,
Moths and butterflies to air from ground,
Yes natures cloak is all around.

The Crown

He is the Oak King, mighty and strong,
His reign will last all summer long,
At the midsummer solstice he'll fight for the
crown,
With the Holly King, dressed in his fine autumn
gown.

The Green Man will watch and then tell the trees,
The Holly King's coming, begin to drop leaves,
To make a grand carpet for him to walk on,
For the Oak King is tired, his powers have gone.

The Holly King now, wears the grand crown with
pride,
The plants and the animals hurry to hide,
Away from the cold and harsh winter wind,
They know the Holly King soon will bring.

The Holly King's powers in strength they will grow,
He'll command strong winds to bring ice and
snow,
At the midwinter solstice his powers will peak,
But the plants and the animals will stay fast
asleep.

Refreshed and reborn the Oak King will wake,
The Holly King's crown soon he will take,
The birds will return and joyously sing,
The plants and the animals will welcome the
spring.

Happy again the Green Man will be,
His kingdom released from the cold misery,
Until midsummer solstice again comes around,
And the Holly King once more, will take back the
crown.

Winter's Hand

Winter's shroud soon will pass,
The summer sun will come at last,
Plants will reach into the light,
The summer breeze will warm the night,
But we must await the sun to cast,
For Winter's hand has not yet past.

The Holly King will hold on fast,
He will make this winter last,
He'll send the ice, the snow, the rain,
He'll send the wind to blow again,
Frozen lakes and frozen lands,
He'll keep us all in Winter's hand.

But fear ye not, his time is short,
The Oak King will soon make him abort,
His mission to bring about misery,
With his icy hands on you and me,
Then we'll rejoice to see at last,
Winter's hand, returned to the past.

Mother Nature (turns the wheel)

Heather on the moorland,
Roses in the yard,
Hear the bird song greet the dawn,
If you wake up with the lark,
Mother Nature turns the wheel,
If you look then you will see,
That there's a place for everything,
From the oak to the bumble bee.

Rivers feed the oceans,
The tides will ebb and flow,
Silver beads will quench our thirst,
And help all things to grow,
Mother Nature turns the wheel,
She gives her time for free,
And brings the joy of her embrace,
To folks like you and me.

Listen in the morning,
Look throughout the day,
Mother Nature's working hard,
To bring good things our way,
It may not be a pot of gold,
Her gift we cannot spend,
But Mother Nature turns the wheel,
And all her love she'll send.

Be one with Mother Nature,
She'll hold you in her arms,
Be at peace with the trees and fields,
With the animals and the plants,
For Mother Nature turns the wheel,
She'll provide all that you need,
And you will live in harmony,
Like the mighty oak and the bumble bee.

Forest Walk

Walking through the forest,
Admiring the scene,
I came across a clearing,
With different shades of green,
On the edge a Silver Birch,
And there a might Oak,
Looking very splendid,
In their autumn coats.

I stood within this clearing,
Surrounded by the trees,
And heard sweet voices singing,
Bringing natures sounds to me,
A squirrel sat upon a branch,
And looked as if to say,
I hope that you enjoy your walk,
This fine autumnal day.

A little further on my walk,
And there in front of me,
Were ponies and herd of deer,
Roaming wild and free,
If there's one wish that I could make,
I'd wish that I could stay,
Surrounded by this natural world,
The remainder of my days.

Green Man

Walk beneath the leafy boughs
Of dear old friends I've known so well
Who shelter the plants, the grass the fern
I'm known as Cernunnos, Pan or Herne

You may see my face in the evergreens
Or peering out from mighty trees
My kingdom stretches across the land
I'm the horned god, I am the Green Man

In thicket, copse, forest or wood
In hedgerows around your neighbourhood
You'll see me if you care to look
Or maybe beside a babbling brook

I am the spirit that covers the land
I have been here since the Earth began
I'm The Horned God, Cernunnos, Herne or Pan
I am the Earths gardener, I AM the Green Man!

Misty Morning

I see the misty morning,
Through eyes still full of sleep,
I see the dampness on the ground,
And trees that seem to weep,
And somewhere high above the mist,
Where the sky is clear and blue,
The sun will try to send a kiss,
Of warmth to me and you.

I see the misty morning,
As I step out of my door,
I wrap myself against the damp,
And the coldness of the floor,
The birds are calling to the One,
Please lift this mist of gloom,
They, like me, just want the sun,
To lighten up my mood.

I see the misty morning,
Creeping oh so silently,
Across the fields and meadows,
And gently hugging me
I feel the coldness of its kiss,
And it's touch upon my sleeve,
And I know that I will surely miss,
The misty morning when it leaves.

Spring

When ice melts on the hilly slopes,
The rivers will swell, and begin to grope,
Their winding journey to the sea,
Past open fields where winter's been.

Past tall trees now bearing leaves,
Past soft grass of vivid green,
Over rocks where snow has been,
The watery convoy heads downstream.

Animals wake from winter sleep,
And from their beds they stiffly creep,
Into the golden springtime sun,
Once more to walk, once more to run.

The sky above, no longer grey,
The sun God sends his golden rays,
As winter retreats and disappears,
And in the woods, the Green Man cheers.

All that live upon this land,
Rejoice to see that winter's hand,
Has been returned into the past,
For spring is here, again, at last.

Autumn

The ferns and flowers are in retreat,
Golden leaves fall at my feet,
It's autumn time and the woodland knows,
Winters hand will soon bring snow.

The Oak King now has lost his crown,
And the Holly King begins to strut around,
Migrating birds now fly away,
But they'll return in springtime days.

Trees quite soon will look so bare,
For winter gales they must prepare,
And the Green Man tends the evergreens,
Severe, harsh winters, he has seen.

We, as humans, will close our doors,
And watch the gales and rain that pours,
And we'll feel safe within our shell,
As those outside are facing hell.

But autumn is a magical time,
Walk the woods and you will find,
The changing colours of the leaves,
As the Green Man steps between the trees.

Though the sun is weakened in the sky,
There's natural beauty to please the eye,
And Pagans give thanks the whole year through,
For what the Goddess gives to me and you.

Spirit of Night

Tired body, heavy eyes,
Silver lights in a midnight sky,
Lay your head on pillows deep,
Drift into the world of sleep.

A different world where dreams abound,
A strange new world, no touch no sound,
There you'll dwell till the morning light,
Safe within the Spirit of Night.

The Wiccan Witch

The Wiccan Witch is kind and fair,
Her love for nature everywhere,
She's guided by the spirits high,
And sees the world through caring eyes.

The Wiccan Witch thanks all around,
The Green Man here upon the ground,
The spirits that rise into the air,
The Wiccan Witch will truly care.

The Wiccan Witch will celebrate,
And to the God and Goddess will dedicate,
Her offerings and her joyous praise,
And ask for guidance on her way.

The Wiccan Witch will fill your heart,
And from her love, you'll never part,
But on you a spell has not been cast,
You've been guided by spirits, so bound to last.

The elements from the Earth and Air,
Has set you on the path to where,
You'll find your Wiccan Witch to be,
It's true my friends, it's happened to me.

Glorious Autumn Day

I rested on a fallen branch,
In the middle of no-where,
A silent wind kissed the leaves,
And stirred the morning air,
The song of birds came to my ears,
And then I saw a Jay,
And a woodpecker that was very near,
Tapped a welcome to the day.

From my fallen branch I saw,
A rippling stream close by,
Above the water, back and forth,
Were colourful Damsel flies,
And as the morning sun shone through,
The autumn leaves above,
I thought that here dreams can come true,
One can easily fall in love.

Upon my fallen branch I sat,
Not sure how long I stayed,
But realised that the bright blue sky,
Had turned to clouds of grey,
Even though the sun had left,
And the wind had turned quite strong,
This place I thought was still the best,
With its stream and sweet bird song.

The time had come for me to leave,
This wonderful resting place,
Reluctantly I sadly heaved,
My pack and began to pace,
But one last look for memories,
Before I walked away,
So I can recall in the winter freeze,
This glorious autumn day.

Children Of The Earth

We know they feared our Pagan ways,
They tried to wipe us out,
They tortured and they burned us,
If they had the slightest doubt,
They took away our festivals,
Replaced them with their own,
But we stood strong and carried on,
We've flourished and we've grown.

They said we worshipped Satan,
Stole babies and much worse,
And if by chance someone fell ill,
They said we laid a curse,
They took us in for "questioning",
Tortured till we confessed,
But anyone would say the words,
Under such duress.

With bodies bruised and broken,
They put us on the stand,
The priests said we'd offended God,
And the devil took our hand,
The villagers believed them,
Our guilt was their desire,
Then everybody turned out to see,
The witch burned in the fire.

They never really understood,
And some to this day still,
Do not understand our craft,
We bear no one ill will,
We live a life of peace and love,
At one with Mother Earth,
So in secrecy the Hedgewitch lives,
Gathering berries, leaves and herbs.

I sometimes think that there are those,
Who live in those dark times still,
They do not wish to understand,
And I guess they never will,
But Pagans all around the world,
Are proud to carry on,
We practice the oldest religion,
In our deeds and in our song.

Be joyful all ye Pagans,
For the road has been so long,
Remember the innocent martyrs,
That suffered in those days gone,
Give your praise to all the Gods,
And the Goddess of rebirth,
For they can never destroy our faith,
We are the children of the Earth.

Arianrhod

High above the earth each night,
You bathe us in your silver light,
With gentle wings you heal the weak,
And solace give to those who seek.

Into a large owl you can change,
And see our souls so dark and strange,
For we are mortal, weak and frail,
Be we old or young, woman or male.

On your Oar Wheel you carry the dead,
To Emania where you let them rest,
Then send them back to Earth again,
Once more to walk in the company of men.

As mother, maiden or aged crone,
You watch the world from your silver dome,
We see your beauty and silently nod,
Our mortal thanks to Arianrhod.

Sad Farewell

So now our trip is over,
We've spent one final night,
In the forest of our dreams,
Beneath the stars so bright,
We sadly pack away our things,
For soon we must depart,
And say farewell to this tranquil place,
With sad and heavy hearts.

We've woken every morning,
To skies so clear and blue,
To songs of birds high in the trees,
And squirrels chattering too,
But now there is just silence,
It's as if they seem say,
Thank you for your company,
We're sad you're on your way.

The skies that were so very blue,
Have turned to clouds of grey,
And even the dampness of the dew,
Attempt to make us stay,
But we must depart this special place,
Of magical forest ways,
But we have made a solemn oath,
To return again one day.

Spirits

Morning spirits bring the light,
In darkness spirits guard the night,
They're with you each and every day,
And try to guide you on your way.

They're never seen and seldom speak,
But whisper to you in your sleep,
They may appear within your dreams,
And guard you from the things unseen.

Walk your path, be straight and true,
The spirits are there for me and you,
So harm thee none says the Wiccan Rede,
May the spirits grant your every need.

When you pass to the Summerland,
The ancient spirits will take your hand,
And when I pass, they'll take mine too,
Then forever I'll watch over you.

Silver Moon

Silver moon in a blackened sky
The lady watches from on high
The Goddess calls out 'Come to me'
She calls to those who still believe

Praise her in the full moon rite
Her glow will lighten up the night
The water that her light will kiss
Will give you strength and love and bliss

But hide the water in early morn
let not the rays of a fresh new dawn
Destroy the magic held within
And let the sun god's time begin

Though god and goddess are lovers high
And chase each other around the sky
On Earth their magic cannot meet
But in the heavens they love so deep

Natures Sound

In quiet solitude I sat,
One sunny afternoon
The bees were dancing with the plants,
Dressed in their summer bloom,
Above, the birds put on a show,
Of ariel delight,
I thought how wonderful it must be,
To be a bird in flight.

In quiet isolation,
One warm and starry night
I saw the moon rise high above,
So full, so clear, so bright
A bat swooped by and twisted,
Hunting hawk moths just by sound
As the moon cast silver shadows,
Across their battle ground

In silence in my garden,
Away from bustling crowds,
I listen very closely,
To natures different sounds,
Singing birds, croaking frogs,
Hedgehogs rustling leaves,
And all the while the unseen wind,
Brings new scents home to me.

If there's one wish that I could make,
And knew it would come true,
It would be to share this paradise,
With someone just like you
We'd watch as natures tendrils,
Crawled across the ground
And we would be forever lost,
In the magic of natures sounds

Silver Goddess

Created with love on the edge of time
The Silver Goddess so beautifully fine
Her hair of stars and eyes so bright
She bathes the land in her soft moonlight

Lovers caress in her tender glow
She touches hearts and helps love grow
Her magical fingers will touch you too
Her light is her gift to me and you

So when the full moon begins to rise
This Silver Goddess with sparkling eyes
Bathes this land with beams of love
In silent thanks you'll look above

Unconscious though your glance may be
You'll look in wonder and you'll see
Her eyes are looking back at you
And the smile that says "This light is for you"

Halloween

Don't walk out alone tonight,
For something prowls in the soft moonlight,
Something sinister, something strange,
Something that's known by several names.

There in the shadows with blazing eyes,
Or behind a hedgerow it may lie,
Footsteps closing you may hear,
You turn around but no-one's there.

A chilly wind blows this night,
Blood curdling scream gives a fright,
And there behind a garden wall,
Are ghostly figures standing tall.

Tonight you know as Halloween,
When the dead rise up and can be seen,
Perhaps they are just passing through,
Or maybe they have come for you!

Witches, Warlocks, Wizards too,
Black cats, watching every move,
Ghastly ghouls will roam tonight,
Apparitions dance in ghostly flight.

Dressed as children they will be,
Knocking on doors this Halloween,
So don't walk out alone tonight,
Take children with you, you'll be alright!

The Owl

Known in certain circles,
As the cockerel of the night,
A guide they say to the underworld,
With its very keen eyesight,

Arianrhod, the moon goddess,
Shapeshifts into this,
Bringing comfort to the weak,
And solace to those who seek,

With its large all seeing eyes,
She looks into the darkened soul,
And sees the lie that's hiding there,
In the blackness where it grows.

The owl is wise and moon magick,
Is associated with this bird,
A symbol of death and renewal,
And to fear it is absurd.

A swift and silent hunter,
The owl is mighty fine,
Her hooting in the night will say,
I'm with you for all time.

Young Sun God

The young Sun God, now reborn,
Sends the rays to gently warm,
The frozen soil upon the Earth,
And we rejoice at his rebirth.

We know his strength will grow and grow,
And leafy buds begin to show,
Upon the branches of the trees,
Where the icy hand of winter's been.

The icy sheets upon the lakes,
Scream in protest as they break,
Under the gentle springtime sun,
And winters demons are on the run.

Springtime bulbs raise their heads,
Awakened from their sleepy beds,
By the call of Earth's Green Man,
And soon their flowers will proudly stand.

The forests and hedgerows come alive,
As burrowing animals no longer hide,
Beneath the hard and frozen land,
As the Holly King now loosens his hand.

The young Sun God will soon retake,
His rightful crown and he will make,
The Earth once more a glorious place,
And his smile will show on everyone's face.

Now is the time we celebrate,
The Sun Gods return to his heavenly state,
And he will dance in his ballrooms on high,
And to the Holly King we say goodbye.

My Pagan Wish

How many feet have trodden this path,
I wonder as I walk,
How many folk have passed this way,
How many have stopped to talk,
Did they dwell in huts of mud,
Or fashioned from the trees,
Did they live in harmony,
Or were they forced to leave.

Did they live in Pagan times,
Performing rituals in these woods,
Did they celebrate the sun,
With friends who understood,
Did they live a peaceful life,
At one with living things,
Or were they persecuted,
For all that they believed.

I would give most anything,
To stay here for all time,
To live among majestic trees,
Suits my pagan soul just fine,
With nature I would be at one,
In peaceful harmony,
I'd always know the moon and sun,
Would shine their light on me.

But I am not that fortunate,
To the city I must return,
Back to the cold uncaring streets,
Where people never learn,
Back to the place where no one cares,
Where nothing's really fine,
I wish my pagan soul could live,
In this forest for all time.

An it Harm None

This world would be a better place,
If everyone believed,
The pagan rule of bring no harm,
To those who live and breath,
But that's an idealogoly,
That can never be fulfilled,
For religions all around the world,
Bear other faiths I'll will.

They all say they are peaceful,
They say their God is right,
They say that if you don't believe,
You should forfeit your life,
Just look back at history,
And even here today,
Religion is not peaceful,
No matter to whom you pray.

A world without religion?
That's never going to be,
For faiths will fight to put their God,
On the pinnacle of the tree,
And if there's no religion,
What then will man fight for?
For man must fight for something,
He must always be at war.

You know my friends, it seems to me,
That whatever you believe,
We only want to live in peace,
But that will never be,
For God will be on both sides,
Fighting against himself,
And we are mere pawns in His game,
His game of cat and mouse.

But we could thwart His little game,
If we only had the will,
To turn our back on evil things,
And bear no one I'll will,
Following the pagan way,
With nature we'd be one,
And we would praise the morning dew,
And the setting of the sun.

Wicca Man

Let's sing songs to the Wicca Man,
In thanks for the harvest yield,
Let's sing songs to the Wicca Man,
Now we've ploughed the fields.

Let's give praise to the Wicca Man,
Make offerings from our fare,
Let's give praise to the Wicca Man,
So he may take our prayers.

Let's give thanks to the Wicca Man,
See how tall he stands,
Let's give thanks to the Wicca Man,
Made from our own fair hands.

Let's set fire to the Wicca Man,
Let us dance and sing,
Let's set fire to the Wicca Man,
And let life again begin.

Let's sing songs for the Wicca Man,
His ashes we will spread,
Let's all praise the Wicca Man,
Now the Wicca Man is dead.

Aeolus

Wild or gentle, soft or strong,
He'll carry the sound of natures song,
He may moan in the hills,
Or whisper in trees,
Give us many thrills,
In his warm calming breeze.

He can never be captured, tamed or calmed,
He can never be taught to bring peace or harm,
He can never be held by women or man,
He will always be free to roam through the land.

He is a part of the great wheel of life,
His breath is the breeze that cools us at night,
His roar is the hurricane, a tornado his grin,
Aeolus is the mighty god of the wind.

Artemis

Artemis the great goddess,
Diana as also known,
Huntress and protector,
In the forests she does roam,
The sister to Apollo,
Her twin it has been sworn,
Her parents Zeus and Leto,
Upon Delos she was born.

One day she sat on Zeus's knee,
And asked for wishes six,
Though Artemis was only three,
Her mind was firmly fixed;
A virgin she would always be,
By many names be known,
And ruler of the mountains she,
With arrows and a golden bow.

Sixty daughters of Okeanos,
To forever be aged nine,
So that they could be her choir,
And live a life divine,
Twenty Amniside Nymphs she wished,
Her handmaidens them to be,
To watch her dogs and golden bow,
While she rested worry free.

A gift to Artimes from Pan,
Seven bitches and six dogs,
And through the forests they all ran,
In sunshine or in fog,
She captured six gold horned deer,
To pull her chariot of gold,
She would always have them near,
And never to grow old.

Artemis the young goddess,
And huntress so divine,
A knee length tunic is her dress,
Her dogs stay at her side,
This is the story I believe,
As told in ancient times,
Of a young girl of only three,
Who became a goddess so divine.

The Gods of Olympus

The gods of Olympus, now there's quite a few,
So take this quiz, and see how you do,
I wonder how many of these you may know,
If you know them all you can certainly crow.

Zeus of course, the king of the gods,
Artemis the huntress, hunts with her dogs,
Aphrodite for love, her beauty so fair,
And look in the sea, Poseidon is there.

Hades resides in his underworld court,
Ares the war god and of battles fought,
The Goddess Demeter, the harvest she looks on,
And Apollo for music and of the sun;

Hera for family, Zeus's wife so divine,
Dionysus the joyful Goddess of wine,
Hephaestus? Well, metallurgy is his sole domain,
And Hermes is the cunning God of all trade.

That just leaves Athena who watches the arts,
And finally Hestia, the Goddess of hearth,
Now that makes fourteen, I said there's a few,
Close your eyes and recall them, how did you do?

Upon Mount Olympus, where they all reside,
Just twelve will stay there at any one time,
Who is your favourite, but whoever you choose,
I hope ALL the gods will watch over you.

Athena

She sprang full grown in armour from Zeus,
His favourite child is she,
The virgin goddess of reason and arts,
Who favours the olive tree.

She invented the bridle, the yoke and the flute,
The ship and the rake and the plow,
She is wise, she is strong, of impeccable repute,
And her favourite bird is the owl.

Greece has a city they've named after her,
Athens is what it is called,
And there you will find the Goddess Athena,
In statues so proud and so tall.

CPSIA information can be obtained
at www.ICGtesting.com
Printed in the USA
LVHW021125240522
719597LV00008B/278

9 781503 097599